A TRUE BOOK™

W9-BUI-557

DISCARD

Experiments With Rocks and Minerals

CAROL HAND

Children's Press®
An Imprint of Scholastic Inc.
New York Toronto London Auckland Sydney
Mexico City New Delhi Hong Kong
Danbury, Connecticut

Content Consultant
Suzanne E. Willis, PhD
Professor and Assistant Chair, Department of Physics
Northern Illinois University
DeKalb, Illinois

Library of Congress Cataloging-in-Publication Data

Hand, Carol, 1945–
    Experiments with rocks and minerals/Carol Hand.
        p. cm.—(A true book)
    Includes bibliographical references and index.
    ISBN-13: 978-0-531-26348-8 (lib. bdg.)   ISBN-13: 978-0-531-26648-9 (pbk.)
    ISBN-10: 0-531-26348-7 (lib. bdg.)   ISBN-10: 0-531-26648-6 (pbk.)
    1. Rocks—Experiments—Juvenile literature. 2.
Minerals—Experiments—Juvenile literature. I. Title. II. Series.
    QE432.2.H354 2012
    552.0078—dc22   2011009399

All rights reserved. Published in 2012 by Children's Press, an imprint of Scholastic Inc.
Printed in China 62
SCHOLASTIC, CHILDREN'S PRESS, A TRUE BOOK, and associated logos are trademarks and/or registered trademarks of Scholastic Inc.

1 2 3 4 5 6 7 8 9 10 R 21 20 19 18 17 16 15 14 13 12

Find the Truth!

Everything you are about to read is true **except** for one of the sentences on this page.

Which one is **TRUE**?

T or F Most rocks are a mixture of minerals.

T or F Most minerals are a mixture of crystals.

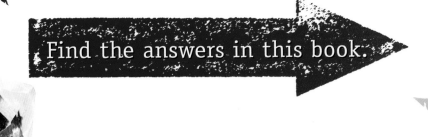

Find the answers in this book.

Contents

Obsidian

You will need to collect some rocks before doing the experiments in this True Book.

Rock layers in the Grand Canyon are hundreds of millions of years old! ➤

Buildings are often made from rock found in the surrounding landscape.

The Science of Rocks

A geologist is a scientist who studies Earth, including rocks and minerals. Scientists are like detectives. They are curious about the world. They ask questions and solve problems by using the scientific method. They observe and collect data. Data are facts or information that relate to a question. Scientists figure out what the data mean. Sometimes they set up an **experiment**, or test, to answer a question.

Granite, sandstone, and limestone are common building materials.

How It Works

This is how the scientific method works. First, a scientist pulls together all the observations about something. Next, he or she thinks up a question that the observations don't explain. Then the scientist forms a **hypothesis**. This is what the scientist believes is the correct answer to the question. It must be a statement that can be tested. Next, he or she plans out an experiment to test it.

Scientists take careful notes as they conduct experiments.

Geologists who study volcanoes are known as volcanologists.

Geologists often need to climb rocks and mountains.

During the experiment, the scientist writes down everything that happens. Finally, the scientist looks at how the experiment turned out and draws a **conclusion**.

Sometimes, the conclusion is that the hypothesis is correct. Other times, it turns out that the hypothesis was not correct. Then it's time to come up with a new hypothesis and design another experiment.

A fossil is the body or imprint of an ancient organism preserved in rock.

A Geological Hypothesis

After observing rocks, one question might be, "How can rocks be classified?" To make a hypothesis, think of logical ways to answer this question. You might say, "Rocks can be classified by color." Then you test this hypothesis. You try to separate rocks into groups based on color. You reach a conclusion: "Yes, rocks can be classified by color" or "No, rocks cannot be classified by color."

First, You Must Collect Some Rocks

To do the experiments in this book, make a collection of rocks and minerals. Look for small chunks, gravel-size or a bit larger. Look for different colors, textures, and patterns. *Always be sure you get permission to take samples!* You can look in places like gravel driveways and shorelines, or in rock or aquarium shops.

You will need to collect some rocks to do the experiments in this True Book. You can find rocks almost anywhere.

CHAPTER 2

A Rocky Rainbow

Many rocks appear gray or brown. Others have bright chunks or stripes of color. Some are black, reddish, or clear. What makes rocks different colors?

Each color in the rock is a mineral. All rocks are made of one or more minerals. Minerals are natural, nonliving substances. They have a **crystal** structure. Some minerals are metals such as copper. Others are gems such as diamonds. Others are substances we use every day, such as salt.

Rock Properties

A property describes an object. You can observe or measure it. Geologists look at several properties of a rock or mineral to identify it. One example is its crystal color, the color it appears to be. Geologists also look at the color of the streak the mineral makes when rubbed on tile. A mineral's luster is also important. Luster is the way light reflects off of a surface.

Rocks can be grouped together according to several different properties.

Demonstration: Rocks' Crystal Colors

Make a copy of the table below in a notebook. You will use this table to record your observations. You may need to add more groups or rock numbers, depending on your rock collection.

Materials:

- **your collection of different kinds of rocks (p. 11)**
- **notebook**
- **pencil**
- **masking tape**
- **note cards**
- **marker**

A data table organizes your data.

Rock Group	Rock Number	Crystal Color	Streak Color
A	1		
	2		
	3		
B	1		
	2		
	3		
C	1		
	2		
	3		

Procedure:

1. Separate the rocks in your collection into solid and multicolored piles. These are your crystal colors.

2. Label each group of rocks A, B, and so on, using note cards. Label each rock in each group 1, 2, 3, and so on, using tape.

3. Record the crystal color or colors of each rock in each group on your table. Leave the Streak Color column blank for now.

Observe: Rocks come in a variety of colors. Different types of rocks can have the same crystal color.

Step 2

What happened? Several different minerals can have similar colors. A single mineral, such as sulfur, can also appear in more than one color. Rocks often have impurities, or different substances mixed in, which can change their appearance. To learn more, a geologist must dig deeper.

Experiment #1: A Brilliant Streak

Observe: Rocks have crystal colors and patterns.

Research question: Does streak color tell a geologist about what a rock or mineral is?

Remember to write down your observations!

A   B   C   D

16

True Book hypothesis: Rocks and minerals can be classified by streak color.

Materials:

- **pencil, notebook, your table with the blank streak column, and your rock collection from the demonstration (p. 14)**
- **ceramic or other rough piece of tile**

Procedure:

1. Scrape your rocks against the tile one by one. Press hard enough to make a streak.

2. Record each rock's streak color in the Streak Color column on your table.

3. Regroup your rocks according to streak color. Relabel the rock groups and numbers in their new groupings.

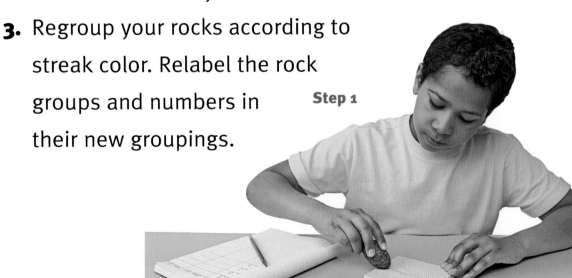

Step 1

17

4. Create a second table, using the one below as an example. You might have to add or take away some rows for your new groupings. Record the rock groups and numbers in their new groupings.

Record your results: Do any rocks look the same but have different streak colors? Are your rocks grouped together differently?

Conclusion: A mineral's streak color is always the same. A geologist can be more sure of what a mineral is by looking at its streak color. Does this match your observations? Was the True Book hypothesis correct?

Rock Group	Rock Number	Streak Color	Crystal Color
A	1		
	2		
	3		
B	1		
	2		
	3		
C	1		
	2		
	3		

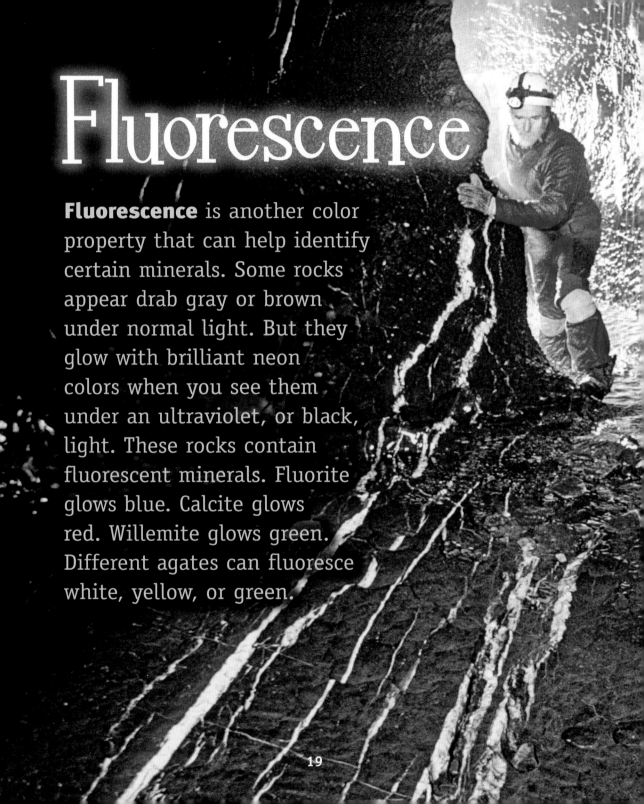

Fluorescence

Fluorescence is another color property that can help identify certain minerals. Some rocks appear drab gray or brown under normal light. But they glow with brilliant neon colors when you see them under an ultraviolet, or black, light. These rocks contain fluorescent minerals. Fluorite glows blue. Calcite glows red. Willemite glows green. Different agates can fluoresce white, yellow, or green.

Breaking Down Crystals

All matter is made of tiny parts called atoms. Atoms fit together to form molecules. Each mineral has only one type of molecule. These molecules fit together in patterns called crystals. Each mineral has a unique crystal shape. Its crystal grows at specific angles, which causes it to break, or cleave, the same way every time. Some crystals are shaped like cubes, and some are six-sided hexagons. Others have more complicated shapes.

Quartz

Each side of a crystal is called a face. Each face is set at a precise angle from the other faces. You can identify a crystal by measuring the angle between its faces.

Granite

Obsidian

Greenstone (Metamorphosed basalt)

Large crystals form when rock such as granite cools slowly underground. Minerals in rock form tiny crystals when lava cools very quickly aboveground. This kind of rock is called basalt. Obsidian is one kind of rock that has no crystals.

CHAPTER 3

Hard as a Rock

Are all rocks equally hard? In 1822, Friedrich Mohs set up a scale based on 10 common minerals to test this question. Each mineral can scratch the one below it on the scale. The softest mineral on Mohs' scale is talc, which forms talcum powder. The other nine minerals will scratch talc. Diamond is the hardest mineral. It will scratch all nine of the other minerals on the scale.

We still use Mohs' hardness scale today.

How Hard?

Fingernails, pennies, and nails have the same hardness as certain minerals. Your fingernail has a hardness of 2.5 on Mohs' scale. Pennies have a hardness of 3.5. A steel nail has a hardness of 5.5. We can use these items to test rock and mineral hardness.

Experiment #1: Scratch

Make a copy of the table below in your notebook. Use the table to record your observations in the next two experiments.

Rock Group	Rock Number	Fingernail (2.5)	Penny (3.5)	Steel Nail (5.5)	My Rock's Hardness
A	1				
	2				
	3				
B	1				
	2				
	3				
C	1				
	2				
	3				

Observe: Some minerals are softer than others.

Research question: Which are the softest minerals?

True Book hypothesis: Some rocks in your collection can be scratched with a fingernail.

Materials (for Experiment #1 and Experiment #2):
- **your rock collection, as grouped in the previous table (p. 18)**
- **penny**
- **steel nail**
- **your table (p. 23)**

Gather these materials.

Step 2

Procedure:

1. Try to scratch each rock with your fingernail.

2. If you can see a scratch, write "yes" in the Fingernail column on the table. If not, write "no."

Record your results: Which rocks in your collection were scratched?

Conclusion: Your fingernail will scratch minerals with a hardness of 1 or 2. Does this match your observations? Was the True Book hypothesis correct?

Experiment #2: Harder and Harder

Observe: Some minerals are harder than a fingernail.

Research question: How much harder are these minerals?

True Book hypothesis: Pennies can scratch some rocks in your collection. Harder rocks can be scratched by nails.

Procedure:

1. Try to scratch each rock with the penny. If you can see a scratch, write "yes" in the Penny column on your table. If not, write "no."

Step 1

2. Try to scratch each rock with the steel nail. If you can see a scratch, write "yes" in the Steel Nail column. If not, write "no."

Record your results: Were those rocks the nail could scratch also scratched by the penny?

Conclusion: A penny has a hardness of 3.5. If your fingernail could not scratch a mineral but a penny could, the mineral's hardness is in between. This is around 3. A nail has a hardness of 5.5. It can scratch rocks with a hardness of 5 or less. Were any minerals scratched by the nail but not the penny? These minerals have a hardness of about 5. Does this match your observations? Was the True Book hypothesis correct?

Step 2

27

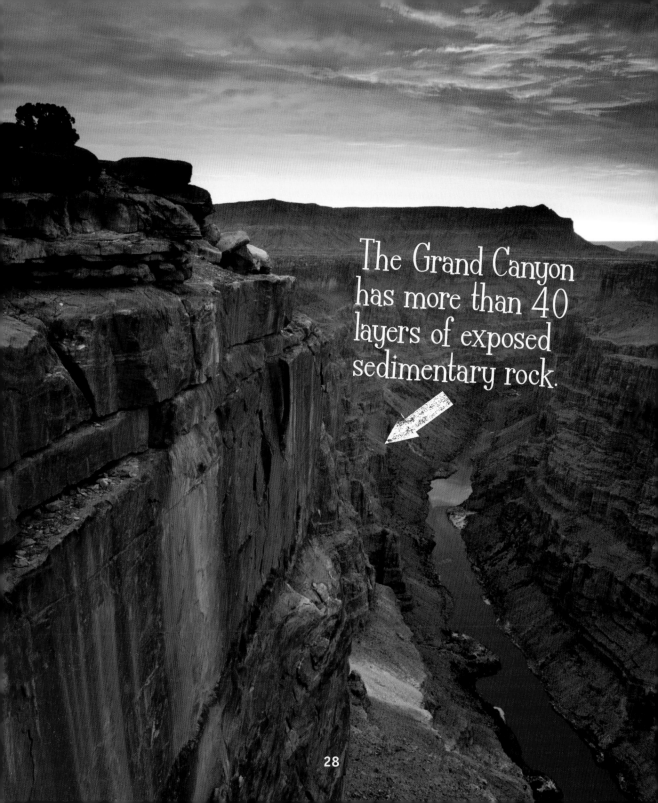

The Grand Canyon has more than 40 layers of exposed sedimentary rock.

Earth as a Rock Factory

Have you ever wondered how rocks are made? **Sedimentary** rock is one type of rock. It is made from sediment, consisting of loose materials such as sand, clay, and gravel that wash downhill and are covered with water. To form rock, sediments must stick together and harden.

Demonstration: Make a Model

Sedimentary rocks form in layers. To get an idea of how this happens, you can make a model. Small seashells can represent fossils.

Materials:

- large, empty plastic bottle
- plaster of paris
- small seashells
- water
- sand
- small pebbles
- gravel
- soil

Procedure:

1. Ask an adult to help you cut off the top of the plastic bottle.

2. Mix equal amounts of dry plaster of paris and sand.

3. Pour the mixture into the bottle to make a layer about 1 inch (2.5 centimeters) thick.

4. Add water to cover the layer. Let the layer harden.

5. Repeat steps 2 through 4, replacing sand with pebbles, then gravel, then soil. Add seashells to make fossils.

6. Add layers until you fill most of the bottle.

Step 5

30

Observe: Your model has layers of rock, just as sedimentary rock does.

What happened? As each layer settles, another layer forms on top. The rock is built layer upon layer.

Experiment #1: Under Pressure

Observe: Each layer of rock adds weight and pressure to the layers below it.

Research question: How does pressure affect rock formation?

True Book hypothesis: Pressure causes sedimentary rock to form into distinct layers.

Materials:
- **large piece of aluminum foil**
- **3 crayons of different colors**
- **knife or crayon sharpener**
- **heavy book**

Do you have everything you need for this experiment?

31

Procedure:

1. Ask an adult to help you chop or shave the crayons into small pieces.

2. Layer the crayon pieces on the foil, one color at a time.

3. Record how the layers look: can you tell where each layer begins and ends?

4. Fold the foil over the layers of crayon pieces.

5. Set a book on top of the foil and press down hard.

6. Carefully open the foil.

Timeline of Grand Canyon Rocks

1,675 millions of years ago (MYA)
The Vishnu schist, the oldest exposed layer, forms.

1,500 MYA
The Zoroaster granite forms above the Vishnu schist.

Record your results: Can you tell where each layer begins and ends?

Conclusion: The weight of each layer above forces the sediment below closer together. Does this match your observations? Was the True Book hypothesis correct?

What happens in nature? Sedimentary rocks form because of pressure. More layers form with time. This adds more weight. Eventually, the sediment layers below harden into solid rock.

500 MYA
The Tapeats sandstone forms. It is now in the center of the canyon.

270 MYA
The Kaibab limestone forms. This is now at the canyon rim.

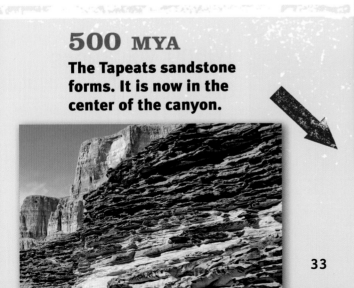

Metamorphic and Igneous Rock

Shale is a sedimentary rock. The deepest layers of shale are at very high pressures and temperatures. They eventually form an entirely new rock called slate. It is a **metamorphic** rock.

Deep inside Earth, high temperatures and pressures melt all minerals and metals. This molten material, called magma, sometimes erupts from a volcano. Magma that reaches the surface is called lava. Lava hardens to form **igneous** rock.

Igneous rock forms as lava cools and hardens.

Many volcanoes are located along the Ring of Fire in the Pacific Ocean.

Rock Drippings

Caves are formed with the help of water. When water seeps into the ground, it often travels through limestone. The water dissolves calcite in the limestone and becomes acidic. The dissolved calcite is carried away with the water. Eventually, the dissolving limestone forms large caves. Sometimes calcite deposits stick to the ceiling of a cave. As water drips over the deposit, a stalactite forms. When calcite drips to the ground and builds up, it forms a stalagmite. Stalactites and stalagmites often form strange-looking cave sculptures.

CHAPTER 5

Earth as Recycler

Huge rocks constantly break down into smaller parts. Over time, they become sand and clay particles. This is called **weathering**. This sediment washes downhill, or **erodes**. It eventually forms new sedimentary and metamorphic rocks. Igneous rocks also break down and make new rocks. This process of constantly making, weathering, and reusing rock materials is called the **rock cycle**.

 Devils Tower in Wyoming is 1,200 feet (366 meters) tall.

Experiment #1: Weathering Rocks

Observe: Limestone is a sedimentary rock made of calcium carbonate, or calcite. Calcite is often made from the shells of tiny marine animals. It has a hardness of three, so it is soft. Limestone weathers easily because it has calcite. This calcite also reacts to acids, such as vinegar.

Research question: Do any of the rocks in your collection contain limestone?

True Book hypothesis: Some of the rocks in your collection contain some limestone.

You will need these materials for the experiment.

Materials:

- **vinegar**
- **eyedropper**
- **magnifying glass**
- **any rocks from your collection with a hardness of 3**
- **any more rocks you think might contain calcite**

Procedure:

1. Use the eyedropper to put 1 to 2 drops of vinegar on one rock.

2. Look at the rock with the magnifying glass.

3. Repeat steps 1 and 2 for each rock.

Step 1

Record your results: Did any bubbles form?

Conclusion: Vinegar reacts with calcite in the rock and breaks it down. This creates bubbles. If a rock produced bubbles, it contains calcite. This means it contains limestone. Does this match your observations? Was the True Book hypothesis correct?

How Much?

Some limestone includes other minerals, such as iron. It can also contain sand or clay particles. This makes limestone harder. Chalk is a soft kind of limestone. Chalk is almost pure calcite. This purer calcite weathers very easily.

Experiment #2: How Much Calcite?

Make a copy of the table on page 40 in your notebook. You will use this table to record your observations in this experiment.

Observe: Some of your rocks may have produced a lot of bubbles. Others produced only a few.

The White Desert in Egypt is filled with formations of easily-weathered chalk.

Research question: How much calcite do my rocks contain?

True Book hypothesis: My rocks contain less calcite than a piece of chalk.

Materials:

- **piece of calcite (calcium tablets from the grocery or drug store, or chalk from a science supply store)**
- **the rocks from the previous experiment (p. 38) that contain calcite**
- **kitchen scale**
- **vinegar**
- **2 glass jars**

Gather these materials.

Test Material	Before Weight	After Weight (oz.)
Calcite		
Unknown Rock 1		
Unknown Rock 2		
Unknown Rock 3		

Procedure:

1. Weigh each rock, including the calcite, on the scale. Record the information.
2. Fill both jars halfway with vinegar.
3. Place the calcite in one jar and the other rocks in the other jar.
4. Let the jars sit overnight.
5. Pour the liquid out of the jar with the calcite.
6. Remove any calcite that remains and leave it to dry.
7. Remove the other rocks from their jar and dry them.
8. Weigh each rock again and record their weights.

Step 2

41

Record your results: Which rocks lost the greatest amount of weight?

Conclusion: Rocks with the greatest difference between their Before and After Weights have the largest amount of calcite. The chalk or calcium tablets you tested should be either mostly or completely dissolved. Does this match your observations? Was the True Book hypothesis correct? ★

What do the rocks look like the next day?

True Statistics

Number of known minerals: 4,000

Number of rock-forming minerals: 20, but only 10 of them make up 90 percent of Earth's crust

Number of minerals contained in a typical television set: 35

Age of oldest known rock on Earth: 4.26 billion years

Age of oldest human-made stone structure: 23,000 years

Weight of world's largest diamond: 1.33 lbs. (0.6 kg)

Weight of rock collection brought back from the moon: 841 lbs. (381.5 kg)

Largest gold nugget ever found: 158 lbs. 13 oz. (72.03 kg)

Did you find the truth?

T Most rocks are a mixture of minerals.

F Most minerals are a mixture of crystals.

Resources

Books

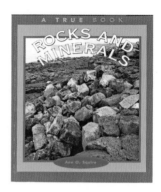

Hoffman, Steven M. *Weathering and Erosion: Wearing Down Rocks*. New York: PowerKids Press, 2011.

Kurlansky, Mark, and S. D. Schindler (illustrator). *The Story of Salt*. New York: G. P. Putnam's Sons, 2006.

Mattern, Joanne. *Minerals and the Rock Cycle*. New York: PowerKids Press, 2005.

Pellant, Chris. *Granite and Other Igneous Rocks*. Milwaukee: Gareth Stevens Publishing, 2007.

Pellant, Chris. *Marble and Other Metamorphic Rocks*. Milwaukee: Gareth Stevens Publishing, 2007.

Squire, Ann. *Rocks and Minerals*. New York: Children's Press, 2002.

Tomecek, Steve, and Kyle Poling (illustrator). *Everything Rocks and Minerals*. Washington, DC: National Geographic Society, 2010.

Organizations and Web Sites

Mineralogy 4 Kids

www.minsocam.org/msa/k12/k_12.html

Learn about mineral groups, properties, crystal structures, and minerals in your home.

RocksForKids

www.rocksforkids.com

See color photos of rocks, minerals, and fossils, and learn how they're formed.

Places to Visit

Crater of Diamonds State Park

209 State Park Road
Murfreesboro, AR 71958
(870) 285-3113
www.stateparks.com/crater_of_diamonds.html

Prospect for diamonds and other types of rocks and minerals, including agate, amethyst, jasper, garnet, and quartz.

Rice Northwest Museum of Rocks and Minerals

26385 NW Groveland Drive
Hillsboro, OR 97124
(503) 647-2418
www.ricenorthwestmuseum.org

See a collection of crystals from around the world.

Important Words

conclusion (kuhn-KLOO-zhun)—final decision

crystal (KRIS-tuhl)—the pattern of molecules that creates the structure of a mineral

erodes (i-RODEZ)—gradually wears away because of water or wind.

experiment (ik-SPER-uh-ment)—a test to try out a theory or to see the effect of something

fluorescence (flu-RES-ens)—the bright light or glow produced by certain rocks and minerals under certain lighting

hypothesis (hy-PAH-thuh-siss)—a prediction that can be tested about how a scientific experiment or investigation will turn out

igneous (IG-nee-us)—a type of rock formed by volcanic activity

metamorphic (met-uh-MOR-fick)—a type of rock formed from other rocks by high pressure and temperature

rock cycle (ROK SYE-kuhl)—process by which rocks are made, broken down, and re-formed into new rocks

sedimentary (sed-uh-MEN-tuh-ree)—a type of rock formed when layers of sand, clay, or other rock materials are cemented together under pressure

weathering (WETH-er-ing)—a process by which rocks break apart over long time periods

Index

Page numbers in **bold** indicate illustrations

About the Author

Carol Hand is a science writer specializing in earth, life, and environmental science. She has a doctorate in marine ecology from the University of Georgia, and has worked as a college teacher, test writer, and curriculum specialist, as well as an author. She has written on various earth science topics, including rocks, weather, astronomy, and oceanography.

PHOTOGRAPHS © 2012: Alamy Images: 10 (Avico Ltd), 32 right (Tom Bean), 20 bottom right, 21 bottom (Susan E. Degginger), 22 (Phil Degginger), 19 (Chris Howes/Wild Places), 8 (Ronald Karpilo), 5 bottom, 33 right, 33 left (Timothy Mulholland), 3, 21 top (Martin Novak), 21 center left, 43 (science photos), 34 (Stocktrek Images, Inc.), 11 (Jack Sullivan); Carol Hand: 48; iStockphoto: 13, 20 background, 21 background, 28; Ken Karp: back cover, 5 top, 15, 16, 17, 24, 25, 26, 27, 30, 31, 37, 38, 40, 41, 42; Photo Researchers, NY: 4, 21 center right (Joel Arem), 36 (Francois Gohier), 32 left (William H. Mullins), 35 (Francesco Tomasinelli); Scholastic Library Publishing, Inc.: 44; ShutterStock, Inc.: 6 (Nana Lau), 39 (Isabella Pfenninger), cover bottom left (Kompaniets Taras), cover (Triff); Superstock, Inc./All Canada Photos: 9.

Experiments with Rocks and Minerals

How long have humans used rocks for building?

The oldest known rock structure is a 23,000-year-old wall in Greece.

INSIDE, YOU'LL FIND:

★ How geologists use rocks and minerals to learn about Earth's history;

★ Experiments, a timeline, photos— and what rocks are made of;

★ Surprising TRUE facts that will shock and amaze you!

ALL **NEW** ALL TRUE!

Children's Press®
an imprint of

■ SCHOLASTIC

www.scholastic.com/librarypublishing

U.S. $6.95

ISBN-13: 978-0-531-26648-
ISBN-10: 0-531-26648-6

9 780531 266489

Experiments With Electricity

The spiral light bulb was invented in 1976.

SUSAN H. GRAY

■ SCHOLASTIC